cupcakes

Ivy Press

cupcakes

25 mouthwatering recipes

Gina Steer

First published in 2008 by

Ivy Press

The Old Candlemakers

West Street, Lewes

East Sussex BN7 2NZ, UK

www.ivy-group.co.uk

ISBN-13: 978-1-905695-72-0

ISBN-10: 1-905695-72-1

Printed in China

10 9 8 7 6 5 4 3 2 1

Ivy Press

This book was conceived, designed
and produced by Ivy Press.

Creative Director Peter Bridgewater
Publisher Jason Hook
Editorial Director Caroline Earle
Art Director Clare Harris
Senior Editor Lorraine Turner
Senior Art Editor Sarah Howerd
Project Designer Kate Haynes
Publishing Assistant Katie Ellis
Concept Design 'Ome Design
Photographer Jeremy Hopley
Food Stylist Susanna Tee

contents

introduction

There is nothing quite like a tray of freshly baked cupcakes to evoke memories of childhood and cherished family moments. Now these little cakes are enjoying a new vogue and are more popular than ever.

It all began in the United States in the early nineteenth century. The first cupcakes were hailed as revolutionary: they needed far less time to bake than a traditional large cake, and were much more portable. But how did they get their name? One theory suggests it was because the ingredients were measured out in cups; another says that their name arose because they were originally baked in cups in the hearth ovens used at that time. Whichever is right, these popular classics have gone on to delight children and adults for generations.

Today the cupcake has returned to the culinary stage in new and exciting ways. It has become playful, trendy and glamorous, with shapes and decorations to suit all kinds of occasions, from dinner parties and birthdays to weddings and Valentine's Day celebrations. There has never been a wider range of possibilities. For example, you can buy cupcake pans in different shapes, such as hearts, butterflies, snowmen or trains. You can ice and decorate cupcakes in myriad ways. You can even layer your cupcakes in a 'tree' for a stunning wedding centrepiece.

You can also vary the shape of a cupcake simply by the amount of batter you put in the cup. Half-fill it, and you will have a flat cupcake, ideal for adding fancy decorations that won't fall off. Fill it to about two-thirds full, and you will have a cupcake baked in the conventional shape, with a surface that has ever-so-slightly risen. Fill it to three-quarters full, and during baking your cupcake will rise over the edge and expand outwards.

Cupcakes are also convenient to store. They will keep for several days in the refrigerator. Alternatively, leave them undecorated and freeze them. In many cases you can also make the icing in advance and freeze it separately. When you are ready to use them, simply defrost, decorate and enjoy!

the basics

To guarantee perfect cakes every time you bake, it is important to observe a few basic principles. There are also some key pieces of equipment you will need in your kitchen.

You probably already have in your kitchen much of the equipment that you will need. However, if you need to buy some of it, none of the items mentioned here are expensive and they are all easily found in kitchen equipment shops, supermarkets and markets, and also through mail order and internet shopping.

You will need a mixing bowl large enough to take all the ingredients comfortably – about 2.5 litres/4½ pints is good – and a smaller one – about 1 litre/1¾ pints – for making icing. Use a wooden spoon for beating: the handle should be of a reasonable length; a child will need a shorter handle. A metal tablespoon or spatula is ideal for folding in flour.

Other useful equipment includes a muffin tin and paper cases for baking and serving cupcakes. Prepare them for the oven before you start mixing ingredients. You will need a sieve for sifting flour, cocoa powder and icing sugar, and a wire rack for cooling cupcakes straight from the hot oven. A grater is useful for grating citrus rind. Use a pastry brush for apricot glaze and to brush rind off the grater. You will also need a rolling pin to roll out the fondant and marzipan, plus small pastry cutters for cutting out the small fondant or marzipan rounds.

Useful tips

• Read the recipe through before starting to bake. That way, all the equipment and ingredients can be gathered before baking so there is no danger of getting halfway through a recipe and discovering that a vital ingredient is missing.

• Always measure your ingredients carefully. Use accurate scales: these are vital for successful baking. If the proportions of ingredients are wrong, the finished result will not be good. In the same way, a measuring jug is essential for the liquids used, and cook's measuring spoons will ensure the right amount of each ingredient is used.

• Place your mixing bowl on a damp cloth to prevent it from moving around when you are beating ingredients, and use a spatula to scrape round the bowl so that none of the mixture is wasted when transferring it to paper cases.

• For the recipes in this book, the white and flowery cases used are smaller cases, while the silver and gold cases are slightly larger. A muffin tin is best for holding the cases because it will help keep the cakes straight during baking. A bun tin will work but will not always keep the cakes straight, and some mixture may overflow.

a feast of cupcakes

cupcake classics

chocolate

citrus

cherry

coffee

mocha

vanilla

minty choc

little princess

contemporary twists

apricot

banana

mango

toffee fudge

french fancy

choc-vanilla

banoffee

cupcake sensations

poppy seed

black forest

tiramisu

strawberry

raspberry

cranberry

birthday celebrations

mother's day

wedding day

easter

chocolate cupcakes

Delicious and easy to make, these will quickly become a firm family favourite. To ring the changes, try making them with milk chocolate and decorating them with white chocolate.

you will need

85 g/3 oz plain dark chocolate, broken into small pieces

115 g/4 oz unsalted butter, softened

115 g/4 oz caster sugar

2 medium eggs, beaten

115 g/4 oz self-raising flour, sifted

3 tbsp ground almonds

2 tbsp cocoa powder, sifted

dark chocolate curls, to decorate

for the icing

115 g/4 oz plain dark chocolate

40 g/1½ oz unsalted butter, softened

1 tsp golden syrup

1 Preheat the oven to 180°C/350°F/Gas Mark 4, 10 minutes before baking. Line a muffin tin with 12 paper cases. Put the dark chocolate pieces in a bowl with 25 g/1 oz of the butter over a saucepan of gently simmering water. Heat until the butter and chocolate have melted. Remove from the heat, then stir until smooth and allow to cool.

2 Cream the remaining butter with the sugar. Gradually beat in the eggs, adding a spoonful of flour after each addition. When all the egg has been added, add the remaining flour, and the ground almonds and cocoa powder and stir lightly.

3 Spoon the mixture into the paper cases, filling them three-quarters full. Bake in the oven for 18–20 minutes, or until cooked and a skewer inserted into the centre comes out clean. Remove from the oven and leave until cold.

4 For the icing, melt the chocolate with the butter and golden syrup in a heavy-based saucepan over a gentle heat. Remove and stir until smooth and blended. Leave until cold.

5 Beat the icing with a wooden spoon until thick, then use to cover the tops of the cakes, swirling the icing. Sprinkle over the chocolate curls and serve.

citrus cupcakes

When using citrus fruits for baking, look for organic varieties. These have not had the skin coated in wax, which is used to make the fruit more attractive. Keeping the fruits in the refrigerator will lengthen their shelf life.

makes 10–12

you will need

115 g/4 oz unsalted butter, softened

115 g/4 oz caster sugar

1 tbsp finely grated orange rind

1 tbsp finely grated lime rind

2 medium eggs, beaten

115 g/4 oz self-raising flour, sifted

3 tbsp ground almonds

2 tbsp lemon curd

pieces of crystallised lemon, lime and orange, to decorate

for the icing

140 g/5 oz icing sugar, sifted

3 tbsp good-quality (thick) lemon curd

2–2½ tbsp lemon juice, strained

1 Preheat the oven to 180°C/350°F/Gas Mark 4, 10 minutes before baking. Line a muffin tin with paper cases.

2 Beat the butter, caster sugar and the orange and lime rind until creamy. Gradually beat in the eggs a little at a time, adding a spoonful of flour after each addition.

3 When all the egg has been added, stir in all the remaining flour and then the ground almonds and lemon curd. Stir the mixture lightly together.

4 Spoon the mixture into the paper cases, filling them three-quarters full. Bake in the preheated oven for 20 minutes, or until cooked and a skewer inserted into the centre comes out clean. Remove from the oven and leave until cold.

5 When ready to decorate, sift the icing sugar into a mixing bowl and stir in the lemon curd. Gradually add the lemon juice a little at a time, mixing to form a coating consistency. Use to spread over the tops of the cakes. Place a piece of crystallised fruit on top and serve.

cherry cupcakes

The combination of cherries with almond is one that no one can resist. To ensure that the cherries do not sink to the bottom of the cakes, wash the cherries thoroughly after chopping, then dry and toss in a little flour.

you will need

115 g/4 oz glacé cherries

85 g/3 oz self-raising flour, sifted

115 g/4 oz unsalted butter, softened

115 g/4 oz caster sugar

1 tsp almond extract

2 medium eggs, beaten

6 tbsp ground almonds

1 tbsp cooled boiled water (optional)

glacé cherries and toasted flaked almonds, to decorate

for the icing

225 g/8 oz icing sugar, sifted

3–4 tbsp semi-skimmed milk

few drops almond extract

1 Preheat the oven to 180°C/350°F/Gas Mark 4, 10 minutes before baking. Line a muffin tin with paper cases. Chop the cherries roughly, then rinse them thoroughly and dry on absorbent kitchen paper. Toss lightly in 2 tablespoons of the flour and reserve.

2 Cream the butter, caster sugar and the almond extract until fluffy. Gradually beat in the eggs a little at a time, adding a spoonful of flour after each addition. When all the egg has been added, stir in the remaining flour, and the ground almonds and reserved cherries. Stir the mixture lightly together, adding 1 tablespoon cooled boiled water if necessary, to give a soft dropping consistency. Spoon the mixture into the paper cases, filling them three-quarters full.

3 Bake for 20 minutes, or until cooked and a skewer inserted into the centre comes out clean. Remove from the oven and leave until cold.

4 Sift the icing sugar into a mixing bowl. Gradually mix to a smooth, spreadable icing with the milk and almond extract. Spread over the tops of the cakes. Decorate with glacé cherries and flaked almonds and serve.

coffee cupcakes

When making coffee to use in baking, use freshly made coffee from instant granules or from ground coffee. Leave the boiling water for 1 minute before pouring onto the coffee or the flavour will be spoilt.

makes 10–12

you will need

1 tbsp coffee granules

1 tbsp almost boiling water

115 g/4 oz unsalted butter, softened

115 g/4 oz light muscovado sugar

1 tsp ground cinnamon

2 medium eggs, beaten

175 g/6 oz self-raising flour, sifted

4 tbsp chopped pecans

1–2 tbsp low-fat natural yogurt

pecan halves, to decorate

for the icing

115 g/4 oz unsalted butter, softened

225 g/8 oz icing sugar, sifted

1 tbsp coffee granules

2 tsp almost boiling water

1 Preheat the oven to 180°C/350°F/Gas Mark 4, 10 minutes before baking. Line a muffin tin with paper cases. Dissolve the coffee granules in 1 tablespoon of almost boiling water. Allow to cool.

2 Beat the butter, sugar and the ground cinnamon until creamy. Gradually beat in the eggs a little at a time, adding a spoonful of flour after each addition.

3 When all the egg has been added, stir in the remaining flour then the black coffee and chopped pecans. Stir lightly, adding sufficient yogurt to give a soft dropping consistency.

4 Spoon the mixture into the paper cases, filling them three-quarters full. Bake in the preheated oven for 18–20 minutes, or until cooked and a skewer inserted into the centre comes out clean. Remove from the oven and leave until cold.

5 When ready to decorate, cream the butter and sugar together until light and fluffy. Dissolve the coffee granules in 2 teaspoons of almost boiling water and leave to cool slightly, then add to the icing and beat until smooth. Spread over the tops of the cakes. Decorate with pecan halves and serve.

mocha cupcakes

When melting chocolate, take care that it does not burn or 'seize' – in other words, become grainy due to overheating. If this happens, take it off the heat and stir in a small knob of butter, then stir until smooth.

you will need

85 g/3 oz good-quality plain milk chocolate, broken into pieces

2 tbsp espresso coffee

115 g/4 oz unsalted butter, softened

115 g/4 oz light muscovado sugar

2 medium eggs, beaten

175 g/6 oz self-raising flour, sifted

for the icing

225 g/8 oz golden icing sugar

3–4 tbsp warm water

25 g/1 oz plain chocolate, melted

1 Preheat the oven to 180°C/350°F/Gas Mark 4, 10 minutes before baking. Line a muffin tin with paper cases.

2 Place the chocolate and black coffee in a bowl over a saucepan of gently simmering water. Heat gently until the chocolate is soft. Remove from the heat and stir until smooth. Leave to cool.

3 Cream the butter and sugar together until light and fluffy. Gradually beat in the eggs, adding a spoonful of flour after each addition. When all the egg has been added, stir in all the remaining flour.

4 Spoon the mixture into the paper cases, filling them three-quarters full. Bake in the preheated oven for 18–20 minutes, or until cooked and a skewer inserted into the centre comes out clean. Remove from the oven and leave until cold.

5 To decorate, sift the icing sugar into a bowl and stir in sufficient warm water to give a smooth icing. Use to coat the tops of the cakes. Place the melted chocolate into a piping bag with a fine writing nozzle. Pipe 3–4 lines horizontally across the icing. Drag a skewer through vertically to give a feathered effect. Leave to set.

vanilla cupcakes

Vanilla is available in three forms – extract, essence or a vanilla pod.
The best is a pod, which is often used to flavour sugar or milk for desserts.
Split open the pod, scrape out the seeds and use as directed in the recipe.

you will need

75 g/2¾ oz golden sultanas

2 tbsp orange juice or brandy

115 g/4 oz self-raising flour

3 tbsp ground almonds

115 g/4 oz unsalted butter, softened

115 g/4 oz caster sugar

seeds from 1 vanilla pod or 1 tsp vanilla extract

2 medium eggs, beaten

silver or gold dragées, to decorate

for the icing

115 g/4 oz unsalted butter, softened

225 g/8 oz icing sugar, sifted

1 tbsp single cream

1 tsp vanilla extract

1 Preheat the oven to 180°C/350°F/Gas Mark 4, 10 minutes before baking. Line a muffin tin with paper cases. Place the sultanas in a small bowl and cover with the orange juice or brandy. Leave for 30 minutes, or until all the liquid is absorbed.

2 Sift the flour into a mixing bowl and stir in the ground almonds. Cut the butter into small cubes, add to the flour and rub in until the mixture resembles fine breadcrumbs. Stir in the sugar and sultanas with any remaining liquid, then add the vanilla seeds or extract. Gradually stir in the eggs a little at a time.

3 Spoon the mixture into the paper cases, filling them three-quarters full. Bake in the preheated oven for 18–20 minutes, or until cooked and a skewer inserted into the centre comes out clean. Remove from the oven and leave until cold.

4 For the icing, cream the butter and then gradually beat in the icing sugar with the cream and vanilla extract to form a spreadable consistency.

5 Coat the tops of the cakes with the icing. Sprinkle with silver or gold dragées, then serve.

Minty choc cupcakes

Take care when adding the peppermint essence, especially when using it in the icing, because it can be quite overpowering. If using sprigs of fresh mint as decoration, make sure that they are clean and free from insects.

makes 10–12

you will need

115 g/4 oz plain dark chocolate

115 g/4 oz unsalted butter, softened

115 g/4 oz golden caster sugar

1 tsp peppermint essence

2 medium eggs, beaten

115 g/4 oz self-raising flour, sifted

3 tbsp cocoa powder

mint sprigs and after-dinner mint chocolates, to decorate

for the icing

115 g/4 oz unsalted butter, softened

225 g/ 8 oz icing sugar, sifted

1 tbsp semi-skimmed milk, optional

few drops peppermint extract

few drops green food colouring, optional

1 Preheat the oven to 180°C/350°F/Gas Mark 4, 10 minutes before baking. Line a muffin tin with paper cases. Break the chocolate into small pieces and place in a bowl over a saucepan of gently simmering water. Heat gently until the chocolate is soft. Remove from the heat, then stir until smooth. Leave to cool.

2 Beat the butter and sugar with the peppermint essence until creamy. Gradually beat in the eggs a little at a time, adding a spoonful of flour after each addition. When all the egg has been added, stir in all the remaining flour. Sift the cocoa powder into the mixture with 1 tablespoon of cooled boiled water, if necessary, to give a soft dropping consistency.

3 Spoon the mixture into the paper cases, filling them three-quarters full. Bake in the preheated oven for 20 minutes, or until cooked and a skewer inserted in the centre comes out clean. Remove from the oven and leave until cold.

4 For the icing, cream the butter and icing sugar together until light and fluffy, adding a little milk if necessary. Add the peppermint extract with a few drops of food colouring, if using. Cover the tops of the cakes with the icing, swirling it to give a decorative effect. Decorate and serve.

little princess cupcakes

These pretty little cupcakes will delight any girl: they have a light orange-flavoured sponge topped with white glacé icing and sprinkled with hundreds and thousands, or why not try stencils and **edible lustre powder**?

makes 10–12

you will need

115 g/4 oz unsalted butter, softened

115 g/4 oz caster sugar

1 tbsp finely grated orange rind

2 medium eggs, beaten

85 g/3 oz self-raising flour, sifted

6 tbsp ground almonds

1–2 tbsp orange juice

hundreds and thousands, sugar flowers, or stencils with gold and silver sugar dusting powders, to decorate

for the icing

225 g/8 oz icing sugar, sifted

3–4 tbsp warm water

edible pink food colouring (optional)

1 Preheat the oven to 180°C/350°F/Gas Mark 4, 10 minutes before baking. Line a muffin tin with paper cases.

2 Beat the butter, caster sugar and the orange rind together until creamy. Gradually beat in the eggs a little at a time, adding a spoonful of flour after each addition.

3 When all the egg has been added, stir in any remaining flour together with the ground almonds. Stir the mixture lightly together, adding sufficient orange juice to give a soft dropping consistency.

4 Spoon the mixture into the paper cases, filling them three-quarters full. Bake in the preheated oven for 20 minutes, or until cooked and a skewer inserted into the centre comes out clean. Remove from the oven and leave until cold.

5 When ready to decorate, sift the icing sugar into a large bowl and blend with the warm water. Add a few drops of pink food colouring if using, and spread over the cakes. Decorate with hundreds and thousands, sugar flowers, or stencilled shapes and leave to set.

apricot cupcakes

These cupcakes are highly aromatic due to the inclusion of the cardamom seeds and they are crammed with tender **sweet** apricots. Topped with a cream cheese **icing**, they are ideal for **coffee time**.

makes 12

you will need

6 green cardamom pods

115 g/4 oz unsalted butter, softened

85 g/3 oz light muscovado sugar

2 tsp finely grated orange rind

2 medium eggs, beaten

85 g/3 oz self-raising flour, sifted

55 g/2 oz wholemeal self-raising flour, sifted

85 g/3 oz ready-to-eat dried apricots, finely chopped

1–2 tbsp orange juice

for the icing

175 g/6 oz cream cheese

350 g/12 oz icing sugar, sifted

to decorate

chopped fresh or dried apricots

2 tbsp toasted flaked almonds

1 Preheat the oven to 180°C/350°F/Gas Mark 4, 10 minutes before baking. Line a muffin tin with paper cases. Crack open the cardamom pods and scrape out the seeds inside; reserve 2 pods for the icing.

2 Beat the butter, muscovado sugar, cardamom seeds and orange rind together until creamy. Gradually beat in the eggs a little at a time, adding a spoonful of self-raising flour after each addition. When all the egg has been added, stir in the remaining self-raising and wholemeal flour. Add the apricots with sufficient orange juice to give a soft dropping consistency.

3 Spoon into the paper cases, filling them three-quarters full. Bake in the preheated oven for 20 minutes, or until cooked and a skewer inserted into the centre comes out clean. Remove from the oven and leave until cold.

4 When ready to decorate, beat the cream cheese with the icing sugar until blended, then stir in the reserved cardamom seeds. Top the cakes with the icing. Decorate with the apricots and flaked almonds, then cover lightly and store in the refrigerator until ready to serve.

banana cupcakes

If you love bananas, you will love these cupcakes. Mashed bananas give a wonderful moist texture, and blend well with the cinnamon and desiccated coconut.

makes 12

you will need

1 ripe bananas, about 115 g/ 4 oz peeled weight

2 tbsp lime juice

115 g/4 oz unsalted butter, softened

115 g/4 oz golden caster sugar

1 tsp ground cinnamon

2 medium eggs, beaten

115 g/4 oz self-raising flour, sifted

55 g/2 oz wholemeal self-raising flour

55 g/2 oz desiccated coconut

small piece of fresh coconut, to decorate

for the icing

225 g/8 oz golden icing sugar

3–4 tbsp lime juice

1 Preheat the oven to 180°C/350°F/Gas Mark 4, 10 minutes before baking. Line a muffin tin with paper cases. Chop the banana and place in a small bowl. Add the lime juice and mash until smooth. Reserve.

2 Beat the butter, sugar and ground cinnamon together until creamy. Gradually beat in the eggs with a little self-raising flour. When all the egg has been added, stir in any remaining self-raising flour. Add the wholemeal flour, mashed bananas and the coconut, then stir the mixture lightly together.

3 Spoon the mixture into the paper cases, filling them three-quarters full. Bake for 20 minutes, or until cooked and a skewer inserted into the centre comes out clean. Remove from the oven and leave until cold.

4 For the icing, sift the icing sugar into a mixing bowl. Gradually stir in the lime juice to form a smooth, spreadable icing. Use to coat the tops of the cakes. Remove the hard shell from the coconut if necessary. Using a swivel vegetable peeler, shave off small pieces of the fresh coconut, keeping the brown skin intact if possible. Sprinkle over the icing and serve.

mango cupcakes

When baking, it is always a good idea to collect all the ingredients before starting to cook and to preheat the oven first. This will ensure that the cakes are cooked at the correct temperature in the correct time.

makes 12

you will need

115 g/4 oz dried mango

55 g/2 oz stem ginger

115 g/4 oz self-raising flour, sifted

55 g/2 oz wholemeal self-raising flour

1 tsp ground ginger

1 tsp baking powder

115 g/4 oz unsalted butter, softened

115 g/4 oz light muscovado sugar

2 medium eggs, beaten

1–2 tbsp natural yogurt or buttermilk

stem ginger, to decorate

for the icing

225 g/8 oz icing sugar

2–3 tbsp syrup from jar of stem ginger

1 Preheat the oven to 180°C/350°F/Gas Mark 4, 10 minutes before baking. Line a muffin tin with paper cases. Finely chop the mango and ginger and reserve.

2 Sift the flours, ground ginger and baking powder into a mixing bowl, then tip in any remaining husks from the wholemeal flour.

3 Cut the butter into small pieces, then add to the flour and rub in until the mixture resembles fine breadcrumbs. Stir in the sugar.

4 Stir in the chopped mango and ginger, then gradually beat in the eggs a little at a time. Add sufficient yogurt to give a soft dropping consistency.

5 Spoon the mixture into the paper cases, filling them three-quarters full. Bake in the preheated oven for 18–20 minutes, or until cooked and a skewer inserted into the centre comes out clean. Remove from the oven and leave until cold.

6 When ready to decorate, sift the icing sugar into a bowl and mix to a smooth icing with the ginger syrup. Spread over the tops of the cakes and decorate with small pieces of stem ginger. Once set, serve.

toffee fudge cupcakes

Muscovado sugar helps give these cupcakes their rich toffee flavour.
When stored, muscovado sugar has a tendency to form lumps. For best
results, beat these out before creaming the butter and sugar together.

makes 10–12

you will need

115 g/4 oz soft fudge pieces

**115 g/4 oz unsalted butter,
softened**

**115 g/4 oz light muscovado
sugar**

1 tsp ground cinnamon

2 medium eggs, beaten

**115 g/4 oz self-raising flour,
sifted**

**55 g/2 oz wholemeal self-raising
flour**

½ tsp baking powder

**1 tsp cocoa powder,
to decorate**

for the icing

**175 g/6 oz soft fudge or toffee
pieces, plus extra to decorate**

4 tbsp semi-skimmed milk

280–350 g/10–12 oz icing sugar

1 Preheat the oven to 180°C/350°F/Gas Mark 4, 10 minutes
before baking. Line a muffin tin with paper cases. Chop the
fudge pieces and reserve.

2 Beat the butter, sugar and ground cinnamon together until
creamy. Gradually beat in the eggs, adding a spoonful of
self-raising flour after each addition. When all the egg has
been added, stir in the remaining self-raising flour. Place the
wholemeal flour and baking powder into a sieve and sift into
the mixture. Stir the mixture lightly together, then stir in the
chopped fudge.

3 Spoon the mixture into the paper cases, filling them three-
quarters full. Bake in the preheated oven for 20 minutes,
or until cooked and a skewer inserted into the centre comes
out clean. Remove from the oven and leave until cold.

4 For the icing, melt the fudge with the milk in a heavy-based
saucepan, and stir until blended. Gradually beat in the icing
sugar to give a light and fluffy icing, adding a little boiled
water if necessary. Spread over the tops of the cakes. Dust
with sifted cocoa powder and top with a small piece of fudge
or toffee before serving.

french fancy cupcakes

To decorate these almond-flavoured cakes, vary the fruits according to personal preference and availability. For maximum flavour, try to buy local, seasonal fresh fruits.

you will need

115 g/4 oz unsalted butter, softened

115 g/4 oz caster sugar

1 tbsp finely grated orange rind

2 medium eggs, beaten

55 g/2 oz self-raising flour

200 g/7 oz ground almonds

1–2 tbsp brandy or orange juice

fresh fruits, such as ripe peaches, nectarines, plums or strawberries, to decorate

fresh cream, to serve (optional)

for the topping

6 tbsp apricot jam

1 tbsp orange juice or brandy

1 Preheat the oven to 180°C/350°F/Gas Mark 4, 10 minutes before baking. Line a muffin tin with paper cases.

2 Beat the butter, caster sugar and the orange rind together until creamy. Gradually beat in the eggs, adding a spoonful of flour after each addition. When all the egg has been added, stir in any remaining flour and the ground almonds. Stir the mixture lightly, adding sufficient brandy or orange juice to give a soft dropping consistency.

3 Spoon the mixture into the paper cases, filling them three-quarters full. Bake for 20 minutes, or until cooked and a skewer inserted into the centre comes out clean. Remove from the oven and leave until cold.

4 Heat the apricot jam and orange juice together, then rub through a fine sieve and use to brush the tops of the cakes.

5 Lightly rinse and dry the fruits. If using peaches, nectarines or plums, cut in half, remove and discard the stones and slice thinly. Hull and slice the strawberries into halves or quarters. Arrange the fruits decoratively on top of the cakes and then brush with the remaining apricot glaze. Cover lightly and store in the refrigerator. Serve with cream, if desired.

choc-vanilla cupcakes

These are the ultimate chocolate cupcake, very decadent and certainly a real treat for all chocoholics. When using chocolate for baking, it is important that the chocolate used has at least 70% cocoa solids.

you will need

115 g/4 oz plain dark chocolate, broken into pieces

115 g/4 oz unsalted butter, softened

115 g/4 oz caster sugar

1 tsp vanilla extract

2 medium eggs, separated

115 g/4 oz self-raising flour, sifted

4 tbsp ground almonds

1 tbsp cooled boiled water

white chocolate curls, to decorate

for the ganache icing

140 g/5 oz plain dark chocolate, broken into pieces

150 ml/5 fl oz double cream

1 Preheat the oven to 180°C/350°F/Gas Mark 4,for 10 minutes before baking. Line a muffin tin with paper cases. Place the chocolate in a bowl over a saucepan of gently simmering water and heat until soft. Remove and stir until smooth. Cool.

2 Beat the butter, caster sugar and vanilla extract until creamy. Gradually beat in the egg yolks, adding a spoonful of flour after each addition. When all the egg yolks have been added, stir in any remaining flour and the ground almonds with 1 tablespoon cooled boiled water.

3 Whisk the egg whites until soft peaks are formed, then carefully fold into the mixture and mix lightly together. Spoon the mixture into the paper cases, filling them three-quarters full. Bake for 20 minutes, or until cooked and a skewer inserted into the centre comes out clean. Remove from the oven and leave until cold.

4 For the icing, put the chocolate and cream in a heavy-based saucepan. Heat gently, stirring occasionally, until the chocolate has melted. Remove from the heat and stir until smooth. Leave for at least 1 hour, stirring occasionally, until cooled and thickened. Beat until fluffy, then spread over the cakes, swirling decoratively. Decorate with white chocolate curls, cover lightly and store in the refrigerator until ready to serve.

banoffee cupcakes

Be prepared to make another batch of these yummy cupcakes full of toffee and banana and a hint of chocolate, because they'll disappear quickly! The banana gives them their wonderful moist consistency.

makes 12

you will need

1 ripe banana, approx 115 g/ 4 oz peeled weight

2 tbsp lemon juice

115 g/4 oz unsalted butter, softened

115 g/4 oz light muscovado sugar

1 tbsp finely grated lemon rind

2 medium eggs, beaten

85 g/3 oz self-raising flour, sifted

55 g/2 oz wholemeal self-raising flour, sifted

½ tsp baking powder

chocolate flake, to decorate

for the icing

115 g/4 oz light muscovado sugar

115 g/4 oz unsalted butter, softened

200 ml/7 fl oz condensed milk

1 Preheat the oven to 180°C/350°F/Gas Mark 4, 10 minutes before baking. Line a muffin tin with paper cases. Mash the bananas with the lemon juice and reserve.

2 Cream the butter with the sugar and lemon rind. Gradually beat in the eggs, adding a spoonful of self-raising flour after each addition. When all the egg has been added, sift in the remaining self-raising flour together with the wholemeal flour and baking powder. Stir lightly.

3 Spoon the mixture into the paper cases, filling them three-quarters full. Bake in the preheated oven for 18–20 minutes, or until cooked and a skewer inserted into the centre comes out clean. Remove from the oven and leave until cold.

4 For the icing, place the sugar and butter into a heavy-based, non-stick saucepan and heat gently, stirring, until the sugar has dissolved. Add the condensed milk and bring to the boil, then cook for 3–4 minutes, or until a thick consistency is formed. Remove from the heat and leave to cool until just setting. Beat until fluffy, then spread over the cake, swirling the icing. Crush the chocolate flake, use to decorate the cupcakes, then serve.

poppy seed cupcakes

Poppy seeds have been used in food for over 3,000 years. The tiny black seeds impart a delicious nutty flavour when used in baking. Although they come from the opium poppy, they do not have narcotic properties.

makes 10–12

you will need

115 g/4 oz self-raising flour

55 g/ 2 oz wholemeal self-raising flour

½ tsp baking powder

115 g/4 oz unsalted butter, softened

115 g/4 oz light muscovado sugar

2 tsp finely grated orange rind

2 tbsp poppy seeds

2 medium eggs, beaten

1–2 tbsp orange juice

for the icing

150 ml/5 fl oz double cream

to decorate

shredded orange rind

few poppy seeds

1 Preheat the oven to 180°C/350°F/Gas Mark 4, 10 minutes before baking. Line a muffin tin with paper cases.

2 Sift the self-raising and wholemeal flours and baking powder into a large mixing bowl, and tip any husks remaining in the sieve into the bowl.

3 Cut the butter into small pieces. Add to the flour together with the sugar, orange rind and poppy seeds. Stir lightly.

4 Add the eggs and then, using a hand-held or free-standing mixer, mix for 1–2 minutes until thoroughly blended. Add sufficient orange juice to give a soft dropping consistency.

5 Spoon the mixture into the paper cases, filling them three-quarters full. Bake in the preheated oven for 20 minutes, or until cooked and a skewer inserted into the centre comes out clean. Remove from the oven and leave until cold.

6 When cold, whip the cream until soft peaks are formed and use to cover the top of each cupcake. Decorate with orange rind and poppy seeds and store lightly covered in the refrigerator until ready to serve.

black forest cupcakes

It may seem a little unusual using drinking chocolate in these cupcakes. However, it works well, producing a moist, Madeira-style sponge that is perfect when teamed with cream and dark cherries.

makes 12

you will need

115 g/4 oz unsalted butter, softened

115 g/4 oz caster sugar

2 medium eggs, beaten

115 g/4 oz self-raising flour, sifted

85 g/3 oz drinking chocolate, sifted

1 tsp baking powder

1 tbsp cooled boiled water (optional)

for the topping

1–2 tbsp kirsch or Cointreau, optional

150 ml/5 fl oz whipping cream

to decorate

fresh or canned black cherries

chocolate flake or triangles

1 Preheat the oven to 180°C/350°F/Gas Mark 4, 10 minutes before baking. Line a muffin tin with paper cases.

2 Beat the butter and caster sugar together until creamy. Gradually beat in the eggs a little at a time, adding a spoonful of flour after each addition. When all the egg has been added, stir in any remaining flour.

3 Stir the mixture lightly, then add the sifted drinking chocolate with the baking powder, and 1 tablespoon of cooled boiled water if necessary, to give a soft dropping consistency.

4 Spoon the mixture into the paper cases, filling them three-quarters full. Bake in the preheated oven for 20 minutes, or until cooked and a skewer inserted into the centre comes out clean. Remove from the oven and leave until cold.

5 Sprinkle the tops of the cakes with the kirsch, if using, and leave for at least 10 minutes.

6 Whip the cream until soft peaks are formed and use to cover the tops of the cakes. Decorate with the cherries and either chocolate flakes or chocolate triangles. Cover lightly and store in the refrigerator.

tiramisu cupcakes

If you have a coffee machine that makes espresso coffee, use that for the coffee required in this recipe. Otherwise, look for jars of espresso granules and make as normal. Leave to cool slightly before using.

you will need

1 tbsp espresso coffee,
or espresso granules

2 tbsp brandy

115 g/4 oz unsalted butter,
softened

115 g/4 oz golden caster sugar

2 medium eggs, beaten

115 g/4 oz self-raising flour, sifted

1–2 tbsp low-fat natural yogurt

1 tsp cocoa powder,
to decorate

fresh raspberries, to serve

for the icing

225 g/8 oz softened
mascarpone cheese

225 g/8 oz icing sugar, sifted

1 tbsp brandy

1 Preheat the oven to 180°C/350°F/Gas Mark 4, 10 minutes before baking. Line a muffin tin with paper cases. If using coffee granules, put them in a small jug. Heat the brandy until almost boiling, then pour over the coffee granules. Stir until dissolved. If you are using espresso coffee, add the brandy to it.

2 Beat the butter with the caster sugar until creamy. Gradually beat in the eggs a little at a time, adding a spoonful of flour after each addition. When all the egg has been added, stir in all the remaining flour and then the black coffee and yogurt.

3 Stir lightly together, then spoon into the paper cases, filling them three-quarters full. Bake in the preheated oven for 18–20 minutes, or until cooked and a skewer inserted into the centre comes out clean. Remove from the oven and leave until cold.

4 To make the icing, beat the mascarpone cheese until creamy, then gradually beat in the icing sugar, beating well to remove any lumps. Stir in the brandy. Top the cakes with the mascarpone icing. Dust lightly with sifted cocoa powder. Cover lightly and store in the refrigerator until required. Serve with fresh raspberries.

strawberry cupcakes

When choosing strawberries for decoration, look for tiny ones. Alternatively, choose large ripe strawberries, slice each one from the tip to the stalk without cutting all the way through, then pull gently apart to form a fan.

you will need

6 tbsp good-quality strawberry jam

115 g/4 oz unsalted butter, softened

115 g/4 oz caster sugar

2 medium eggs, beaten

85 g/3 oz self-raising flour, sifted

85 g/3 oz ground almonds

few baby strawberry leaves if available or tiny mint leaves, to decorate

for the icing

150 ml/5 fl oz whipping cream

225 g/8 oz baby strawberries

1 Preheat the oven to 180°C/350°F/Gas Mark 4, 10 minutes before baking. Line a muffin tin with paper cases. Place the jam in a small glass bowl and, using a pair of scissors, chop any large pieces of fruit.

2 Cream the butter and caster sugar together, then gradually beat in the eggs a little at a time, adding a spoonful of flour after each addition. When all the egg has been added, stir in the remaining flour and ground almonds. Gently stir in the strawberry jam.

3 Spoon the mixture into the paper cases, filling them three-quarters full. Bake in the preheated oven for 20 minutes, or until cooked and a skewer inserted into the centre comes out clean. Remove from the oven and leave until cold.

4 When ready to decorate, whip the cream until soft peaks are formed. Cover the tops of the cakes using a knife to make soft peaks in the cream. Decorate with the strawberries, and strawberry or mint leaves. Cover lightly and store in the refrigerator.

raspberry cupcakes

Take care when adding an ingredient to give a rippled effect. Here, simply add the cooled jam and stir gently only once. Spooning the mixture into the cases will also give a rippled effect.

makes 10–12

you will need

175 g/6 oz fresh raspberries

115 g/4 oz unsalted butter, softened

115 g/4 oz caster sugar

1 tbsp finely grated orange rind

2 medium eggs, beaten

115 g/4 oz self-raising flour, sifted

tiny mint leaves, optional, to decorate

for the topping

1 carton (284 ml/10 fl oz) clotted cream

1 Preheat the oven to 180°C/350°F/Gas Mark 4, 10 minutes before baking. Line a muffin tin with paper cases.

2 Reserve half the raspberries for decoration. Place the remainder in a small bowl and crush lightly. If desired, rub through a sieve to remove any pips.

3 Cream the butter, caster sugar and orange rind together, then gradually beat in the eggs a little at a time, adding a spoonful of flour after each addition. When all the egg has been added, stir in any remaining flour.

4 Add the crushed raspberries, then gently stir, creating a rippled effect.

5 Spoon the mixture into the paper cases, filling them three-quarters full. Bake in the preheated oven for 20 minutes, or until cooked and a skewer inserted into the centre comes out clean. Remove from the oven and leave until cold.

6 When ready to decorate, spoon 1–2 teaspoons of the clotted cream on top of each cupcake. Decorate with the reserved raspberries, and mint leaves if using, and serve. Cover lightly and store in the refrigerator.

cranberry cupcakes

If you cannot find self-raising wholemeal flour, use plain and increase the baking powder by one teaspoon. This will lighten the mixture and ensure that the cakes rise well. Once decorated with icing, keep refrigerated.

makes 10–12

you will need

115 g/4 oz self-raising flour

55 g/2 oz wholemeal self-raising flour

1 tsp ground cinnamon

115 g/4 oz unsalted butter, softened

85 g/3 oz light muscovado sugar

55 g/2 oz carrots, peeled weight, grated

55 g/2 oz walnuts, chopped

2 tsp finely grated orange rind

85 g/3 oz dried cranberries

2 medium eggs, beaten

about 1 tbsp orange juice

walnut halves, to decorate

for the icing

185 g/6½ oz cream cheese

350 g/12 oz icing sugar

1 Preheat the oven to 180°C/350°F/Gas Mark 4, 10 minutes before baking. Line a muffin tin with paper cases.

2 Sift the self-raising and wholemeal flours and ground cinnamon into a large mixing bowl, then tip any husks remaining in the sieve into the bowl.

3 Cut the butter into small pieces, then add to the flour and rub in until the mixture resembles fine breadcrumbs.

4 Stir in the sugar, grated carrots, walnuts, orange rind and cranberries. Stir lightly. Then mix in the eggs and enough orange juice to give a soft dropping consistency.

5 Spoon the mixture into the paper cases, filling them three-quarters full. Bake in the preheated oven for 20 minutes, or until cooked and a skewer inserted into the centre comes out clean. Remove from the oven and leave until cold.

6 For the icing, beat the cream cheese and icing sugar together until creamy, then top the cakes with it. Decorate with the walnut halves, cover lightly and store in the refrigerator until ready to serve.

birthday celebrations

You can cook as many or as few of these cakes as you like to make any party go with a swing. They can be stacked on a serving platter and the candles lit. Afterwards, simply put a cake in each take-home goody bag.

you will need

225 g/8 oz unsalted butter, softened

225 g/8 oz golden caster sugar

1 tsp vanilla extract

4 medium eggs, beaten

225 g/8 oz self-raising flour

55 g/2 oz good-quality milk chocolate, grated

8 tbsp ground almonds

1 tbsp cooled boiled water (optional)

cake candles and holders, or halved glacé cherries with candles, to decorate

for the icing

450 g/1 lb icing sugar, sifted

6–8 tbsp semi skimmed milk

pink, blue, green and red edible food colourings, optional

1 Preheat the oven to 180°C/350°F/Gas Mark 4, 10 minutes before baking. Line a muffin tin with paper cases.

2 Beat the butter, caster sugar and vanilla extract until creamy. Gradually beat in the eggs, adding a spoonful of flour after each addition. When all the egg has been added, stir in the remaining flour, grated chocolate and ground almonds, with 1 tablespoon cooled boiled water if necessary, to give a dropping consistency.

3 Spoon the mixture into the paper cases, filling them three-quarters full. Bake for 18–20 minutes, or until cooked. Remove from the oven and leave until cold.

4 For the icing, sift the icing sugar into a mixing bowl. Gradually mix to a smooth, spreadable icing with the milk. Divide into 2–4 small bowls, and stir in a few drops of different coloured food colouring if using. Ice the cakes, then leave to set.

5 Decorate with either cake candles and holders, or a halved glacé cherry with a candle. Light the candles, then serve. Or pipe 'Happy Birthday' in contrasting colours, one letter per cake, or use contrasting coloured icing to coat each cake, then feather with a different colour (see page 20).

mother's day cakes

Here is the perfect way to say, "I love you, Mum!" Light and fluffy, these cupcakes have plenty of chocolate and they are beautifully decorated. Look for a small wicker basket to arrange the cakes in. Perfect!

makes 12

you will need

115 g/4 oz golden caster sugar

115 g/4 oz unsalted butter, softened

2 medium eggs, beaten

115 g/4 oz self-raising flour, sifted

6 tbsp ground almonds

55 g/2 oz good-quality plain dark chocolate, grated

1 tbsp cooled boiled water (optional)

sugar flowers, to decorate

for the icing

115 g/4 oz unsalted butter, softened

225 g/8 oz icing sugar

1 tbsp milk

1 Preheat the oven to 180°C/350°F/Gas Mark 4, 10 minutes before baking. Line a muffin tin with paper cases.

2 Beat the sugar and butter together until creamy. Gradually beat in the eggs a little at a time, adding a spoonful of flour after each addition.

3 When all the egg has been added, stir in the remaining flour together with the ground almonds and grated chocolate. Add 1 tablespoon cooled boiled water if necessary to give a soft dropping consistency.

4 Spoon the mixture into the paper cases, filling them three-quarters full. Bake in the preheated oven for 18–20 minutes, or until cooked and a skewer inserted into the centre comes out clean. Remove from the oven and leave until cold.

5 Cream the butter for the icing, then gradually beat in the icing sugar with the milk to form a spreadable consistency. Pipe on the cakes and decorate with sugar flowers, then arrange in a hand-held wicker basket to serve.

wedding cupcakes

Make these cakes as near as possible to the big day, then store cold in airtight tins to keep them as fresh as possible. If desired, drizzle a little extra brandy or Cointreau over the cakes before icing. Keep them cool.

makes 34–36

you will need

225 g/8 oz dried mango, finely chopped

4 tbsp brandy or Cointreau

350 g/12 oz butter, softened

350 g/12 oz caster sugar

6 medium eggs, beaten

280 g/10 oz self-raising flour, sifted

115 g/4 oz ground almonds

2–3 tbsp semi-skimmed milk

crystallised rose petals or other sugar flowers of your choice, or ribbon bows, to decorate

for the topping

6 tbsp apricot jam

1 tbsp orange juice

675 g/1 lb 8 oz white fondant icing

cornflour, for dusting

1 Preheat the oven to 180°C/350°F/Gas Mark 4, 10 minutes before baking. Line muffin tins with silver paper cases. Place the mango and brandy in a bowl, then leave for 30 minutes.

2 Cream the butter and caster sugar together, then gradually beat in the eggs with a spoonful of flour after each addition. When all the egg has been added, stir in the ground almonds and remaining flour. Stir in the mango, then the remaining brandy with sufficient milk to give a soft, dropping consistency.

3 Spoon the mixture into the paper cases, filling them three-quarters full. Bake in the preheated oven for 18–20 minutes, or until cooked and a skewer inserted into the centre comes out clean. Remove from the oven and leave until cold.

4 For the topping, heat the apricot jam and orange juice together, then rub through a sieve and brush over the cakes. Roll out the icing on a surface lightly dusted with cornflour. Cut out 34–36 rounds measuring 6.5 cm/2½ inches in diameter, then place on top of each cake. Top with crystallised rose petals, other sugar flowers or ribbon bows. Arrange the cupcakes on a cake stand or tray. When the cake ceremony is performed, the bride and groom can hand out the cupcakes on small individual plates.

easter cupcakes

Why not have some fun with these cupcakes for your Easter celebrations, and ask the kids to help? They can use two or three of the easy decorating ideas given below – a perfect way to keep everyone happy.

makes 24

you will need

140 g/5 oz golden sultanas

2 tbsp brandy or lemon juice

225 g/8 oz unsalted butter, softened

225 g/8 oz caster sugar

1 tbsp finely grated lemon rind

4 medium eggs, beaten

185 g/6½ oz self-raising flour, sifted

50 g/1¾ oz ground almonds

small sugared chocolate eggs and/or fluffy baby chick decorations, to decorate

for the topping

2 tbsp apricot jam

2 tsp lemon juice

225 g/8 oz prepared natural or golden marzipan

icing sugar, for dusting

1 Preheat the oven to 180°C/350°F/Gas Mark 4, 10 minutes before baking. Line a muffin tin with paper cases. Cover the sultanas with the brandy or lemon juice. Leave for 30 minutes.

2 Cream the butter, caster sugar and lemon rind until creamy, then gradually beat in the eggs with a spoonful of flour after each addition. When all the egg has been added, stir in the remaining flour with the ground almonds. Stir in the sultanas and soaking liquid.

3 Spoon the mixture into the paper cases, filling them three-quarters full. Bake in the preheated oven for 20 minutes, or until cooked and a skewer inserted into the centre comes out clean. Remove from the oven and leave until cold.

4 For the topping, heat the apricot jam and lemon juice together, then rub through a sieve.

5 Roll out the marzipan on a surface lightly dusted with icing sugar. Cut out 24 star or flower shapes, brush with a little apricot glaze, and place on top of each cupcake.

6 Top with either small sugared chocolate eggs or fluffy baby chick decorations.

decorating ideas

The look of the finished cupcake is so important to the enjoyment of eating them. Food should appeal to all the senses: it should look good, smell good and, of course, taste good.

To ensure maximum pleasure, make your icing the correct consistency. It should cover the cake thickly enough so that the sponge does not show through, but should not be difficult to spread; this applies in particular to glacé icing. Butter cream needs to be soft enough to spread evenly over cakes, allowing it to be gently pulled up into peaks.

Icings can take on any colour with the addition of edible natural food colouring. Stir in the colour very slowly, a few drops at a time. If using for children, check their sensitivity to food colours.

Allowing the icing to set applies in most cases, and particularly when using stencils to decorate the cakes. Stencils can be bought from cookshops and come in a variety of shapes. Being very easy to use, they provide an effective and easy way to decorate the cake. Simply ice the cake and allow to set before placing the stencil in the middle of each cake and then sprinkling over cocoa powder, icing sugar, coloured edible lustre powder, sugar strands, melted chocolate or warm sieved jam. Carefully lift off the stencil and, if necessary, allow to set before serving.

There are many other tricks to help you decorate your cupcakes prettily and professionally. For example, when you are adding a decoration, such as nuts, chocolate shavings, sugar flowers or edible fresh flowers, let the icing set a little but not completely or the decoration will spoil the surface or might just slip off.

When choosing your decorations, simple ingredients can be used. Brush the cakes with apricot glaze and cover with sifted cocoa powder, or try chopped or halved nuts, crumbled chocolate flake, grated chocolate, glacé cherries and angelica leaves, sugar flowers, and hundreds and thousands. Apricot glaze is perfect to finish fresh fruits used as decoration. Apply with a clean pastry brush and allow to set before serving.

index

acknowledgements

Bright Ideas,
38 High Street,
Lewes,
East Sussex
BN7 2LU

Revive-all,
The Old Needlemakers,
West Street,
Lewes,
East Sussex
BN7 2NZ

Steamer Trading,
20/21 High Street,
Lewes,
East Sussex
BN7 2BY

Wickle,
24 High Street,
Lewes,
East Sussex
BN7 2LU